SHADOWS AND
MIRACLES

SHADOWS AND MIRACLES

Poems

Cristina Necula

To order additional copies of this book, contact:
Xlibris Corporation
1-888-795-4274
www.Xlibris.com
Orders@Xlibris.com
38124

Contents

Preface

What is poetry?—a series of rhyming stanzas, a smattering of words, an electric rush of emotion on the page? It is none of these. It is all of these. It is an elusive thing indeed, a tremulous force that speaks to the mind and soul collectively. William Wadsworth described poetry as "the breath and finer spirit of all knowledge." According to Gustave Flaubert, "there is not a particle of life which does not bear poetry within it." Perhaps Muriel Rukeyser put it best when she said: "The sources of poetry are in the spirit seeking completeness." No matter how we choose to define it, here's a point we can all agree on: poetry is powerful.

And so it is with the poems in this volume.

You may not know Cristina Necula personally—I have known her for only a relatively short period of time—but her poems will immediately befriend you. In her imaginative, articulate, and very daring hands, poetry becomes a sort of passport, granting the reader access to a rarefied world. Enter a page here and you will find yourself traveling through a decadent landscape where love and the mysteries of the human heart are explored. Enter a page there and you will find yourself on a mystical journey that speaks directly to the spirit. There is humor in this collection of poems, along with equal measures of candor and wisdom and hope. For all of her versatility as a poet, Cristina Necula manages to keep her inner eye focused on the unique map of the soul, and many of her poems will leave you breathless and aching for more. She isn't afraid to delve into the darkest regions of the human condition, nor is she intent on painting a bright picture of the world around her. These are poems for all walks of life because they spiral through thought and emotion like the wise serpent—at times silently, at times dangerously, cutting across the rich floor of the forest in verdant flashes. You may feel stung and provoked, amused and saddened, aroused and abandoned, but you will always *feel*—and what more can we ask of poetry?

I encourage you to explore this collection of poems with an open mind and an open heart. Read them aloud or to yourself or in the company of friends. Then sit back and treasure the magic of the journey, because that is precisely what Cristina Necula has set out to do here. These poems are an invitation to a place where words glow and descriptions flow, a place where readers will journey to again and again.

Antonio Pagliarulo
New York City
December 2006

Miracle

a cosmic miracle
descended
along the Milky Way

tonight
the light
of your existence
cracked the wall

I heard Jupiter call
my name

you came
in brilliance forceful and kind
you touched my mind

and now my heart
captured
like a bird with frail wings
it sings
no more of freedom
but of love

for it's within the sky
of your treasured soul
that I can fly the highest
of all

November 24, 2006—New York

Photodream

I dreamt I was a photograph

pause

in your dance with the infinite
watching you
paint
distinction
with
equality

humans fabricated in the factory of divine will

one by one
they claim eternity
at the gates of your perception

stop

your eyes swallow patterns
of misery and decadence
within a tender cosmic space

hold
the circle of a moment
uncovering its perfect form

for in your eyes
the dark
holds the promise of truth

October 30, 2006—New York

Woman of Shadows

I stand raw
I lie sacred
I've pressed all the buttons
Just to summon truth naked

Dare to try
And let your instincts fry
Can you feel
The Devil's at your heel

I'm the woman of shadows
Standing right behind you
Don't slip, don't slide, don't cower
One wrong move and I surround you

I lurk in every doubt
I lure you to impasse
I'm crawling through your veins
With a magnifying glass

Drop your weapons
You're no angel
"Cowards die a thousand deaths"
And you're in danger

Routine saves you
Till daylight disappears
I'm the darkest midnight
Of your deepest fears

I'm the woman of shadows
Your subtle provocation
When you're flooded with fear
I reward you with temptation

I'm dancing on your conscience
As you're digging your own hole
Just open your mind, stranger
I'm the mirror to your soul

October 4, 2006—New York

My Lover and My Friend

you are the Force
beneath my secret world

your written words are
all I taste of you now
yet echoes of your soul
break through
your mask of self-defense
and literature . . .

with you
my world has turned
to fire and faith
constant to a dream
that holds too dear
the mystery of you unlived
unloved

I plead with every breath
to let you go
but air itself is vibrant
with your music

you master
all the tantrums of my senses
then hide behind the jealous Moon
who steals your light

I cannot live the fantasies you conquer

already lost in you
my only strength
is that I love
what has not yet been born
of you, my lover and my friend

your Revolution

August 20, 2006—New York

a year without you

time
bends and folds
upon itself
like a paper airplane
in a perpetual return
to its origins

a year without you

a year of reversed
definitions
where silences blush
more
than words

and Thought
is nothing
but a lame excuse
to hold you
deeper

June 1, 2006—New York

Two Seconds Away

'Cause I'm two seconds away from insanity . . .
Pretty girl doing right by humanity,
Got to find the right reasons
To stick to the seasons,
To follow the hours,
Grease polite conversation,
Boycott imagination,
Drown my wit in the role
Of the Venusian whole.

Crush my body,
Starve my mind,
Curse my kind.

My freedom is a mocking jail,
Burden of a crawling snail,
Carry freedom on my back
Like a sordid shell,
A sack
Filled with thoughts of what can be,
Thoughts with ears and tongues
That speak,
Eyes that see beyond the borders
Of paths they are trained
To seek.

I am weary of myself
And the wars I wage,
The rage
To be free yet understood,
To live by decree of "should."

My freedom's a transparent cage
Locked in age
And space and self,

The wings
Are strings
That bind to tease
A flight of immortality.

Please
Let me christen me
Two seconds away from insanity.

May 29, 2006—New York

In Awe

I don't remember when I changed
but I remember you
your friendship and your way

we drove down Broadway on that day
you said it's gonna be okay
and all I did was turn away
to make you stay

you weren't playing any games
no claims
of property or chains

but I was 26 and change
my vision spanned a one-eyed range

you left it lightly
at good-bye
and I
declined
the invitation to be kind

I don't remember all I've torn
but what I can't forget
is when regret
was born

and now you're here
a timid step
away from holding out your hand
to help me stand

March 29, 2006—New York

Identify

My neck is in the noose
And life is floating puzzles . . .
Enigmas on the loose . . .

When preachers end up murdered
And superheroes freeze,
Won't somebody, please
Tell me what's going down?

Will I wake up today
To find my soul on E-Bay
'Cause the Devil's out shopping
And Hell is a park
Where kids dream of candy
And strangers are handy . . .

Look who's missing today . . .
Who is screaming today?
Who is tortured to shreds?
Who is making the beds?
Who lies cold on the floor?
Who is begging for more?

Tell me who . . .
Who are you?

Can't deny that I'm scared,
Can't defend what I claim
Like a sniper prepared
To take an aimless aim.

I don't do anything,
And I say nothing new,
But I want to know who . . .
Who are you?

I can't seem to decide
If it makes sense to hide,
To donate, to defy
Or to cry . . .

Who's infected today?
Who has seen their last May?
Who's the man with the plan
To wipe out a whole clan?

Look who's fighting today
On your 7th birthday,
Bruises and ice cream cones,
Bank accounts, broken bones . . .

Tell me who . . .
Who are you?

March 29, 2006—New York

Evolution

And maybe I can see the truth
When standing at the edge of youth
I cut the chord my mother bled
And fed
A thread
Of Balkan dread.

Ahead
Of chains and absolution
A blackjack crack of evolution
A speed-greed-feed-need-a-solution
To serve the sacred institution
Of man and woman

Woo the man
Wolf down the woman
Wounded plan
Where woman splits
And hits
And grits
Her teeth and ears and tits
And bits
Herself

himself, myself, ourselves,
our shelves
inclined by the caresses we designed
to grind the mind and bind the blind

the Deaf, the Mute, the No, the Why

the Lie

I lie, you lie, he lies with you
He lies alive aligned with you
You lie alight
He lights a plight

And maybe I can let it go
By knowing that I do not know
What, whom or where or when I owe
A No

But it's too late to play the bait
To lie in wait, to rate the fate
And maim the lame . . .

It's blame the shame
And claim the name

My game.

March 27, 2006—New York

The Songwriter's Excuse or Ballad of the Apologetic Poet

Oh, I don't mean to say
That my world is okay,
That my selfishness is blissful
And my midnights are peaceful,

And I don't mean to brag
That I serve my own flag,
That my loyalty's nameless
And my actions are blameless.

But you make me defend
My means to the end
As a preordained pact
Between fiction and fact.

Now, I don't say you belong
To the womb of a song
And I don't mean to boast
That I've used you the most,

But I'm still renting a space
Where cheap posters of your face
Cover cracks in the wall
Of a tenement hall.

I don't want to be mean
'Cause my heart's still sixteen
And I don't seek to imply
That we can't live a lie.

But my pen is a whore,
Flaunting words door to door,
There's no point to repent
'Till all letters are spent.

There's no ink to explain
It's just another missed train.

March 26, 2006—New York

enough

don't wanna know you
don't want your autograph
don't want the letters of your name
in my epitaph

don't wanna please you
lying here in my bed
watching porno flicks and shooting
arrows in my head

oh you're the teacher you're the father
you're the husband you're the brother
you're the son the holy spirit
and your cross is gold

you're talking friendship and religion
like a parrot to a pigeon
and your tongue's a foreign legion
of the lies you've sold

you are the image of perfection
you're society's selection
when morality comes flashing
cameras at your door

but it won't do you any good
to wash your hands and deck your mood
'cause you've saved every soul you could
and yet you're still a whore

don't wanna pay you for your time
don't wanna spare you from your slime
don't wanna be your special friend
don't wanna lie don't wanna bend

you want me but you can't decide
if you're the groom the virgin bride
or if you simply wanna hide
your filth under my dress

"the bitter searching of your heart"
might fall to play a lesser part
'cause you still can't define my art
to fit in your success

don't wanna be here
don't wanna sabotage
the system and the sacred order
of your entourage

don't wanna know you
don't wanna rock your christian soul
don't want your "kodak-moment" life
to fill my existential hole

March 26, 2006—New York

Vision

within a teardrop

I saw the map

the soul's geography

in salty waters drowned

a microscopic universe

of pain

Unbound

The Hourglass Decree

Sweat drips from the hourglass
Weary of serving time . . .

"If the desert should stop
Running through my waist,
The canvas of desire remains blank.

For as the seconds roll
In infinite grains,
The burden of Want
Crucified on the altar
Of ignoble humanity
May not grow heavier than a milligram
Of hour-eating sand."

June 18, 2005—London, England

Mirage

Wind-swept caravans,
Mosaics . . .
The Sultan craves a game of chess.
Pipes of opium-smoke-rising patience
In languorous deliberation . . .

The women sway like tall and supple grass,
The Sultan's hand runs through them,
Intoxication of the captured stranger . . .

Dare to play a game of chess
While subjugation looms.

A fragrance sketched in whiffs of golden dunes
And restless caravans
Who steal my North and South.

Dancing snakes and thieves converge
By the light of the Moon
Unraveling an invitation from the Sultan
To play a game of chess,

I falter
And undress,
In silent expectation of the senses
Suspended by a thread of painful hope . . .

The game begins.

A strategy of thought and patience
Eludes me,

Wrapped in the harem veil,
Swaying like wind-swept grass,
My turn to move.

Queen, pawn, king
In opium illusion
Remain confused and undistinguished . . .

The Sultan watches draped in centuries of patience,
I am undone, my frailties disclosed,
I hold a pawn with future hopes of Queenhood,
But Time is still my enemy,
I cannot nestle my head against its chest
To breathe in my own heartbeats one by one.

The caravans have stopped in the oasis,
Life still pursues the footsteps of the sun,
I play a game of chess where Kings and Fools
Hold lengthy conversations
On topics of conversion and convention.

The Sultan smiles,
I sway like wind-swept grass,
His hand is buried in my silky form
Searching for feeble roots.

I am entangled in a game of chess,
I own no strategies, no centuries, no patience,
The Sultan waits in Victory's sweet arms,

It is my turn to move.

June 7, 2005—London, England

Buttons

I handed him a map;
an electronic board
of soul, body and head.

He looked
He touched
He said:

This button is for laughter
This button is for hope
This button is for tears
This button's for submission

And this button is supposed
To pause your intuition

This button is for love
This button is for pain
This button is for silence
This button is for fear

And this button is supposed
To make you disappear

May 19, 2005—New York

OFF . . .

Galleries of pain;
Artwork swiftly severed
From the decayed carcass
Of some memory.

Eagerness, subside!
Desperation, wither!
Give birth to the hope
Of Eternity.

A collected hunger
For the soul's resources
Pours in through the brittle
Window of self-defeat.

Serving East and West
Platters of cooked pleasure
With a side of wisdom—
An artist in retreat.

Loneliness is riding
On a mighty broom,
Sweeping dust and embers.
Fire will not bloom.

Echo has no tongue
To respond to silence
And the screaming angels
Drive a soundproof taxi.

Help comes with instructions
Of limited usability
And a lifetime contract
Of reversed servility.

Etching letter-portraits
Of gods, idols and enemies,
A service to refusal
Of aged responsibilities.

Weigh blood against desire
And Fear will tip the scale
In favor of Approval—
The Woman's Holy Grail.

My self-expression's loaded
Pointing East and West;
Finger's squirming inside me
Fighting for the trigger.

Inverted alphabets
And good intentions fail.
Feeding on mud and fury,
Does innocence prevail?

May 19, 2005—New York

Indecision

I
Haven't yet said "good-bye"
To this bittersweet lie
Of pretend bliss

I
Crush my hopes into dust
Just to cover the rust
Of your kiss

You
Cause me to reassign
A degree of divine
To your mess

You
Make my atoms surpass
Their intangible mass
Of nuclear stress

We
Are a hazard of choices
Deaf to each other's true voices
Of greed

We
Sing a quartet for two
Two cages in a human zoo
Of primal need

I
Play roulette on my heart
And you're quoting Descartes
To justify

You
Think and therefore you are
But I can't get very far
Past "why"

We
Are a hazard of choices
Deaf to each other's true voices
We're petrified

But I
Haven't yet said "good-bye"
To this beautifully wry
State of mind

October 1, 2004—New York

Brain-Garden

There's magic in the air
In Brain-Garden,
Words sparkle and invent
A new dance.
In sentence chains, they prance
And pour on the White,
They let me write
Tonight.

Last night was Bingo night
In Brain-Garden.
Words played and gained
Too little,
They felt old and brittle,
And weak.
No winning streak.

Tonight is romance night
In Brain-Garden.
Words meet and fall in love,
They please
And stroll with graceful ease.
Letters unite
In satisfactory succession
On the White.

There's magic in Brain-Garden
On the lawn.
The words are gathering
Their brilliant spawn,
Bursting out the Pen-Gate
Onto the White.
They let me write
Tonight.

August 28, 2004—New York

Gypsy Heart

The Southern wind has stirred my longing.
If I could go,
I'd travel far from all belonging
To meet no one I know.

I hear the echo of my sorrows,
It's time to fly,
My heart is bound by your tomorrows
Like a captive sigh.

let me run
the desert simmers in deception
underneath the sun

let me be
release my soul from all conception
unchain me free

You don't have the power
To kill me with kindness,
I'm a gypsy flower,
Wilting in your blindness.

Open the gate,
My heart cannot wait;
It's drunk and it's bait
For madness.

I seek no salvation,
No promise, no lie,
No full transformation
From moth to butterfly.

Don't ever start
To take me apart
In your cerebral art,
You're crushing my gypsy heart.

Your love is buried in deception.

let me be
release my soul from your perception
unchain me free

August 25, 2004—New York

Dream

Eyes of light and fire
In your night attire,
Catch me a dream
From your cosmic stream.

And if I don't
Chase the day,
Let me stray
On your Milky Way.

Dream of hope and wonder,
Tear my world asunder.
Help me conceive
A truth I can believe.

And if I don't
Chase the day,
Let me stray
On your Milky Way.

Spin me in illusion,
Gift of the night,
Deepen my confusion,
Mirage of light.

Spin me in illusion,
Treasure of the night,
Sweeten my confusion,
Dream of light.

August 6, 2004—New York

Beyond Indictment

This morning I employed
A militia of neurons
To stifle the rebellion
Known in less legal terms
As May-dreams of recurring
Obsession.

It happened overnight
In slumbering inattention
With misguided intention:
The rebels penetrated
The inner fortress.

They set up a large screen
Right in the arid middle section
Of the heart battlefield.

All feelings gathered 'round
Amazed at the insurgence,
Spellbound and staring
At the screen.

Your face, your eyes,
Your smile, your hair,
Your nose and lips,
Your feline stare.
You looked a little rounder,
Perhaps older,
But there was nothing new
About you being you.

One by one, the feeling-mother,
The feeling-father and all
The little feeling-children
Carrying your last name,
They came.

Along with great-grandparent-feelings
And revived relative-feelings
Stepping out of their fleshy tombs,
They drew close to the screen
And fell down on their knees,
They held hands and screamed:
"Un-freeze!"
In wild reunion.

Here's Happiness, there's Tenderness;
There goes great-grandma-Love,
Poor old thing long-forgotten,
Dead, buried and neglected,
Now resurrected.

"Alert! Alert!" resounded
In the upstairs lab—
Neurons keeping tab
On internal changes:
"There's mutiny down below!"

The captain-neuron yawned away
A whiff of sorrow:
"I'm sleeping. Let's deal with it
Tomorrow."

This morning I appealed
To the Supreme-Judge-Brain:
"You haven't been informed
Of recent uprisings, it seems.
I call upon you to indict
My dreams."

"You may call your first witness."
Declared solemnly Judge-Brain.

"Your honor, my first witness
Is Pain."

Pain entered the courtroom,
She wore a prickly dress.
She stepped on neurons' toes
And scratched the heart walls
Until she settled down
Somewhere around the nose.

As liquid testimony
Trickled from hazel pools
On each side of the nose,
Pain rose
And said:

"Your honor, I have witnessed
Insurgence last night.
I'm here to testify
On behalf of the plaintiff,
Victim of this sudden
Revolution.
You see, I am both Problem
And Solution.

I have been brought forth
By the rebel fighters
Of the Subconscious Legion.
They screened a film last night
By that twisted director,
Sir Memory
Or something of the kind,
Quite unrefined.

The Feeling-clan was incited
To wild manifestations,
Resurrected, united
In uncanny divinations,
And incantations
Which woke me up
From sweetest slumber.

So, here I am, your Honor.
There's certainly one thing
About which we agree:
I'd rather sleep
And the plaintiff
Wants to be rid of me."

Judge-Brain crackled in static
From Neuron-Jury talk
Trickling down from the cerebral
Attic.

"I've had them all arrested
This morning" said the Judge.
"The Feeling-clan along with
Sir Memory have been
Placed under the strictest supervision.

I still haven't located
The Subconscious Legion,
They're hiding in a deeply
Treacherous region.

But our secret Bureau
Of special neuron agents
Is working on that matter.
Pain, you may step down.
Case is dismissed."

Pain swirled its thorny gown
And scratched the neuron-jurors
In passing.

The jurors were not pleased
With Judge-Brain's quick decision,
They felt he lacked precision,
And hadn't analyzed
All evidence.

The film, for instance,
Should be seen.
They asked for the screen
And watched it several times.

They had Sir Memory brought in
For comment.
Pain re-appeared high
On caffeine.
Unable to sleep, she listened
To the speculation:

What if? What if? What if?

If I had gone, if I had run,
If I had stayed, if I had prayed,
If I had known, if I had shown,
If I had dared, if I had cared,
If I had guessed your bluff,

If I had loved
Enough.

I'll bribe you once again
To allow me to breathe.

But I cannot
Understand
Why you still steal
My May sleep
To hold my hand.

I speak out loud
For fear that
Words of such deadly weight
Might shatter my interior
If not allowed
To leave my lips and poison
My intimate
Exterior.

So, I appealed anew
To the mighty Judge:
"What should I do, Judge-Brain?
The jury has still
Not reached a verdict."

Brain spoke: "They never will.
Hung jury in this case.
But all's under control."

I counter: "Pain is still here."

"Just treat her to a beer
Or some other form
Of fun, involving less
Neuron-assassination."

"And Pain will disappear?"

Judge-Brain is crackling hard:
"There's too much going on!
Sometimes I want to sleep.
You make me work too deep
On internal matters.

I'm happier when I deal
With external affairs.
I'm content when you feed me
Steaks of knowledge
And when you have a date
With Courage.

Use me to use your skills.
Create, and I'll reward you
With immeasurable thrills.

Pain will never leave you,
She might take a nap
Once in a while,
Enough to give you time
To smile.

But she's not all that bad.
Sometimes she makes you drink
Your tears, so you won't sink."

I listened to Judge
And followed his advice.
When Pain sat on my heart,
I didn't budge.

I called Sir Memory
And had a production meeting.
Between the three of us,
Pain, Memory and me,
There's bound to be some creativity
And plenty of delusion.

I thanked Judge-Brain
In a swift medical
Gesture of disposal:
I threw out all the bottles
Lying 'round my bed.
No more neuron murders
Infused in alcohol
And dread . . .

At least within the next
Hours or so.

Tonight I serve my country,
Judge-Brain and Neuron Bureau
And I enlist to Logic.

I strive to serve them well

So that when midnight comes,
I won't regret
When I rebel.

May 15-16, 2004—New York

Impossibility

I find it difficult to give
When you ask
My love to be
A task.

My allergies are acting up
Whenever you fill the air
With constancy perfume
And care.

You love me and I tell myself
The privilege is mine.
Your love is strong
Like twenty year-old wine.

You ask if I still like you
In a 5:00 AM bout
Of sensitivity.
You doubt.

In my adult version
Of Show-and-Tell, I'm proud
To be loved by you
In a crowd.

But I am just a loner
Who belongs to a strange race

In love

With space.

March 12, 2004—Vienna, Austria

Does It Hurt

"I bought a muscle-contracting machine
And used it while I ate,
Taking down my pulse
To check my millionth heart rate."

I asked him: "Does it hurt?"
He said: "Well, not that much.
It's just a form of torture, but not what I'd call pain."

I said: "No! Does it hurt?"
He answered: "Would I lie?"
"NO!" I repeated.
"Does it hurt to die?"

He blinked in green confusion:
"I don't know what you mean.
All I said was:
'I bought a muscle-contracting machine!'"

"What does it do?" I whispered into the tiny ear
Behind the hollow cheek.
"It's just like exercise," he said,
"Without the exercise."

I can't speak.

The snake above his temple to the right
Coils in an infuriated vein,
A taut reminder
Of family genes and self-inflicted pain.

I'm frightened.

In his frenzy
Of antioxidants, electrolytes and fear,
A cry of desperation
Is all I hear.

Cancer and stroke and heart attack,
Cholesterol and bones,
Muscles, intestines, fat
And perfect heart rate zones . . .

I stare at a slave of physical perfection,
Internal and external;

Controlling,
Abstaining,
Restraining,
Refraining,
Conflicting,
Inflicting . . .

Clone of Marquis de Sade,
Reborn to monitor his every profane breath,
Condemned to life
By fear of death.

I'm suddenly awakened
By a consciousness blow:
"His fear of death surpasses mine,
By twenty years or so!"

I want to be consoling
Despite the incontestable cliché
That almost leaves my lips:
we all die someday!

However, I still manage
To maintain my self-respect
And I appeal to his alluring
Intellect:

"My love, we have so much to do,
To taste,
To live,
To breathe, to see . . .
Free."

I kiss his sweaty brow:
"We have so much to be!
Right now."

March 12, 2004—Vienna, Austria

The Unfulfilled

The creature asked for springtime,
The heavens hid the sun.
The creature longed for summer
When winter had begun.

"The night is awfully cold,
And terror floods my brain.
I am a frozen mold
Of never-ending pain."

The creature searched for truth
But Fear blocked its path.
The creature begged for peace;
The world provoked its wrath.

"The night is awfully cold,
My heart, a dried-up well.
I am a frozen mold,
A relic out of hell."

The creature implored Love
When Loneliness set in,
And sold its fragile soul
To gratify its skin.

"Descending into hate,
A mask upon my face,
I am a pawn of Fate
In the absence of grace."

November 13, 2001—New York

Sonnet I

Last night I came upon a thousand sorrows,
They danced beneath my window as I prayed,
They promised me unbearable tomorrows,
And then I knew too well I should have stayed.
Your emerald eyes imprinted in my being
Devour every second of delight.
As lips are made to kiss, so eyes in seeing
That which they've lost, are now blinded by night.
The treasure of your heart I dare not guess
Nor do I venture to reclaim as mine,
I swallow tears and hate and tenderness,
But, at your hand, they are the sweetest wine.

Love is no servant that I dare command.
Come, dear sorrows, help me understand.

May 1, 2000—Vienna, Austria

Sonnet II

Do you intend to melt me with your charm
Or give me hope when my whole world seems vile?
Day after day, I watch how you disarm
My soul of its defenses, with each smile.
A drop of beauty landed on my finger
When my cold hand was conquered by your kiss.
I feared, as I felt your warm lips linger,
That I may sell my freedom for such bliss.
Patience and I have been eternal foes
But what an ally did she find in you!
Thus, of my weapons, I'd gladly dispose
If, in your arms, I could be born anew.

A warrior no more, I bless my fate
For loving you has taught me how to wait.

May 1, 2000—Vienna, Austria

Now

Take this moment of true glory
Wrapped in everlasting light,
Weave the fabric of your story
With each second of delight.

If you weep, cherish your tears,
If you laugh, love every smile.
Frightened? Gather all your fears,
Hold them for a little while.

Should you fall when Love's gate closes
And Pain sings, don't turn away.
In this field of thorns and roses,
Let your soul come out to play.

Leave some questions without answer,
Revel in a fleeting doubt,
Take the hand of that old dancer,
Father Time, and waltz him out.

Breathe in the enchanting spell
Of these moments that go by.
Splendid, horrid—love them well;
They will teach you how to fly.

January 18-19, 1999—New York

One Thousand One Good-Byes

Watching your expression
As you hear my confession
And I want to
Make you cry.
While my imagination
Feeds your anticipation,
Bitter years
Pass us by.

This is no inspiration,
It's just an adaptation
Of ideals
Lost and found.
Conquered by my creation,
You're flirting with temptation
Yet you tend to
Make no sound.

It isn't my intention
To hold hands with convention,
But I'll have to
Let you die.
It's past all comprehension,
This masochist invention
Married to the question "why."

In every complication
There is some innovation
Irresistible to the wise,
Yet through this meditation,
I hand in my resignation,
One thousand one good-byes.

October 4, 1998—Bucharest, Romania